THE STORY OF THE INDIANA PACERS

Roger Brown

Malcolm Brogdon

A HISTORY OF HOOPS

THE STORY OF THE

INDIANA
PACERS

JIM WHITING

T.J. Ford

CREATIVE EDUCATION / CREATIVE PAPERBACKS

Published by Creative Education and Creative Paperbacks
P.O. Box 227, Mankato, Minnesota 56002
Creative Education and Creative Paperbacks are imprints of
The Creative Company
www.thecreativecompany.us

Design and production by Blue Design (www.bluedes.com)
Art direction by Rita Marshall
Production layout by Rachel Klimpel and Ciara Beitlich

Photographs by AP Images (G. Paul Burnett, Michael Conroy, David
Zalubowski), Corbis (Steve Lipofsky), Ebay (kriol7702), Getty (Julio Aguilar,
Mark Bllnch, Dylan Buell, Nathanlel S. Butler, Tlm DeFrlsco, Kevork
Djansezian, Jeff Haynes, Ron Hoskins, Heinz Kluetmeier, Andy Lyons, Manny
Millan, Layne Murdoch, NBA Photos, John Ruthroff, Eliot J. Schechter, The
Sporting News Archive), Newscom (Jim Rassol/abacausa.com), Shutterstock
(Brocreative, Valentin Valkov)

Library of Congress Cataloging-in-Publication Data
Names: Whiting, Jim, 1943- author.
Title: The story of the Indiana Pacers / Jim Whiting.
Description: Mankato, Minnesota : Creative Education/Creative
    Paperbacks, 2023. | Series: Creative Sports. A History of Hoops | Includes
    index. | Audience: Ages 8-12 | Audience: Grades 4-6 | Summary: "Middle
    grade basketball fans are introduced to the extraordinary history of
    NBA's Indiana Pacers with a photo-laden narrative of their greatest
    successes and losses"-- Provided by publisher.
Identifiers: LCCN 2022009472 (print) | LCCN 2022009473 (ebook) | ISBN
    9781640266285 (library binding) | ISBN 9781682771846 (paperback) | ISBN
    9781640007697 (ebook)
Subjects: LCSH: Indiana Pacers (Basketball team)--History--Juvenile
    literature.
Classification: LCC GV885.52.I53 W553 2023 (print) | LCC GV885.52.I53
    (ebook) | DDC 796.323/640977252--dc23/eng/20220224
LC record available at https://lccn.loc.gov/2022009472
LC ebook record available at https://lccn.loc.gov/2022009473

Paul George

CONTENTS

LEGENDS OF THE HARDWOOD

PACING THEMSELVES

Indiana Pacers star shooting guard Reggie Miller was having an off night against the New York Knicks on June 1, 1994. It was Game 5 of the Eastern Conference finals of the National Basketball Association (NBA) playoffs. Miller had made just one of six three-point attempts. Fans heckled him. The rest of his team wasn't doing much better. The Knicks led 70–58 at the end of the third quarter.

As the fourth quarter began, Miller went into "the zone." As NBA.com notes, "It doesn't matter where he catches the ball or how many people are guarding him, once he rises up for the jumper, you just know it's going in." He sank all five of his three-point attempts. That was an NBA record for three-pointers in a quarter. One was an off-balance 27-foot heave. He was 3-for-5 from the two point range. And for good measure, he added four free throws. In all, Miller outscored New York 25–16 by himself in the quarter. His teammates chipped in 10 more points. They won, 93–86.

As the game turned in the Pacers' favor, the heckling stopped. And in the final moments, Miller made a choking gesture towards the fans. It meant that the Knicks gave up a big lead and lost a game that seemed to be well in hand for them.

Reggie Miller

MEL DANIELS | CENTER

MEL DANIELS
CENTER
HEIGHT: 6-FOOT-9
PACERS SEASONS: 1968–74

THE SOFT SIDE OF A TOUGH GUY

When Mel Daniels was a youngster, his mother read
poetry to him. That inspired him to write his own
poems—as many as 20,000! Many had sports themes.
Daniels was secretive about them. He didn't publish any.
He didn't even share them with his teammates. On the
court, he was a daunting opponent. He averaged more
than 19 points and 16 rebounds a game. His greatest
strength was on defense. "I loved to knock guys down,"
he said. Teammate Bill Keller added, "He scared people
out of driving the lane. If he went for a ball and ended
up with someone's head in his hands, he was just as
likely to put a headlock on the guy as let him go."
Daniels was the leading rebounder in ABA history, with
9,494. He is in the Basketball Hall of Fame.

There have been many memorable games like this in the Pacers history, which began over thirty years prior to that night. In the mid-1960s, professional basketball experienced a boom in fan interest. The sport's increasing popularity inspired a group of investors to start a new league called the American Basketball Association (ABA). The Hoosier State of Indiana has always been a hotbed of hoops enthusiasm. The ABA wanted a team in Indianapolis, which is Indiana's largest city.

Team officials settled on Pacers as the name. It honored the pace car that started the Indianapolis 500 automobile race on Memorial Day weekend. The name also paid tribute to harness racing. Horses called pacers pull two-wheeled carts. The jockey sits in the cart and holds the reins. The sport is especially popular in Indiana. The most famous pacer horse, Dan Patch, was originally from the state.

ABA action kicked off in 1967–68. After going 38–40 that first season, the Pacers improved to 44–34 the following season. One key was hiring fiery Bobby "Slick" Leonard as coach. Another was trading for center Mel Daniels. He was the league's Most Valuable Player (MVP). The Pacers advanced to the ABA Finals. They lost to the Oakland Oaks, 4 games to 1. They won a league-best 59 games in 1969–70 and raced to the ABA championship, defeating the Los Angeles Stars in six games.

The Pacers liked to draft players with Indiana connections. They took Rick Mount of Purdue University in 1970. They won 58 games that season but lost in the Western Division finals. After that disappointment, the Pacers drafted Indiana University's George "Baby Bull" McGinnis in 1971. "McGinnis is so strong, you'd swear he weighs 300 pounds," said Willie Wise of the Virginia Squires. McGinnis led Indiana to back-to-back ABA titles.

George McGinnis

JOINING THE NBA

The Pacers fell short of the ABA championship the next three seasons. But they remained competitive even though McGinnis left. Then the ABA had financial problems. It folded after the 1975–76 season. Indiana was one of four ABA teams that joined the NBA.

Indiana had a hard time adjusting to the NBA. The Pacers won only 36 games in 1976–77. One bright spot was the combination of swingman Billy Knight and point guard Don Buse. With Buse feeding him the ball, Knight averaged nearly 27 points a game. "It's because of Buse that I'm having a great year," Knight said. "He'll ask me if there's anything special I want to run. I tell him I'll do something, then I do it, and the ball comes right to me." Both players were selected for the All-Star Game that year.

Indiana traded Knight in 1977. The Pacers posted losing records for the next three seasons. The team made an even worse trade during the 1979–80 season. Small forward Alex English had averaged 16 points the previous season. The Pacers traded him and brought back McGinnis. English went on to score more points than any other player during the 1980s. McGinnis was gone within two years.

Billy Knight

Before he left, McGinnis helped the team to its first NBA winning season in 1980–81. The Pacers fell to the 76ers in the first round of the playoffs. They tumbled to 35–47 the next year. The next four seasons were worse. They didn't win more than 26 games in any of them.

The Pacers made small forward Chuck Person the fourth overall pick in the 1986 NBA Draft. He had been the all-time leading scorer at Auburn University. He became an instant star. He averaged nearly 19 points a game and was named NBA Rookie of the Year. The Pacers went 41–41. They returned to the playoffs for the first time in six years. However, the Atlanta Hawks beat them in the first round, 3 games to 1.

THE FANS AREN'T ALWAYS RIGHT

The Pacers selected shooting guard Reggie Miller in the 1987 NBA Draft. He was one of the best three-point shooters in college basketball history. That didn't matter to Pacers fans. They wanted the team to draft Indiana University guard Steve Alford. Alford had been named Indiana's Mr. Basketball in high school. He went on to become the all-time leading scorer at Indiana. Local fans all knew him by name. "Basically, he owns all of Indiana," a teammate said.

RIK SMITS
CENTER
HEIGHT: 7-FOOT-4
PACERS SEASONS:
1988–2000

WHEN LIFE IMITATES ART

In 1988, Eddie Murphy starred in the comedy *Coming to America*. A scene involved a
basketball game at New York's Madison Square Garden. One team was Marist College.
Moviegoers caught a glimpse of 7-foot-4 Marist center Rik Smits. They weren't the only
ones watching Smits. Pro scouts also had their eyes on him. He impressed them with 24
points in the second half. Like Murphy's character, Smits had also come to America. In
Smits' case, he had come from the Netherlands where he grew up. He was the second
overall selection in the 1988 NBA Draft. He played his entire 12-year career with Indiana.
He ranks second in scoring and third in rebounds.

In contrast, Miller had no local ties. He grew up in Southern California and played for UCLA. Fans booed when the selection was announced. Some doubted if Miller was strong enough to play professional ball. He weighed less than 200 pounds. Miller wasn't an instant success. He came off the bench and averaged just 10 points a game. Alford fans complained. The Pacers went 38–44. Before the next season, they drafted 7-foot-4 Dutch center Rik Smits. They added German-born Detlef Schrempf during the season. But they fell to 28–54 in 1988–89.

The team was poised to do better. Miller finally lived up to expectations in the following season. He averaged more than 24 points a game. The Pacers surged to 42–40. Then the team's progress stalled. They posted almost exactly the same record in the next three seasons. Each time, they were bounced in the first round of the playoffs.

After the 1992–93 season, the Pacers hired Larry Brown as coach. He was a proven winner. He guided Indiana to a 47–35 mark. The Pacers advanced to the Eastern Conference finals. They took a 3–2 series edge. The Knicks won the final two games by close margins. The team had 52 wins in 1994–95. It was their best record in the NBA. The Pacers beat the Knicks in the second round of the playoffs. Indiana faced the Orlando Magic in the conference finals. In a tight series, the Magic emerged with a 4–3 triumph. Three Indiana losses were by five points or fewer. The Pacers won 52 games again in 1995–96. They fell in the first round of the playoffs. The team dropped to 39–43 the following season. Brown left. One legend was gone. Another was about to return.

Detlef Schrempf

INDIANA VS. NEW YORK

EASTERN CONFERENCE SEMIFINALS

GAME 1

MAY 7, 1995

POINTS PER SECOND

With less than 20 seconds left, the Knicks led by six points. Then Indiana's Reggie Miller took a pass and sank a three-pointer. He stole the inbounds pass and scurried back to the three-point line. He whirled around and launched another three-pointer. Nothing but net. The game was tied. A Knicks player missed two free throws. Another tried a short jump shot but it bounced off the rim. Miller grabbed the rebound. He was fouled and then sank both free throws. Game over—Pacers 107, Knicks 105. In the last nine seconds, Miller had scored eight points. "The Knicks, New York, and Madison Square Garden bring out the best in me," Miller said. "It lights a fire inside of me."

INDIANA PACERS

BIRD FLIES BACK TO THE COOP

Larry Bird replaced Brown as coach in 1997. Bird became a legend during his college career at Indiana State University. He enjoyed a great pro career with the Boston Celtics. After he retired, he was eager to return to Indiana. Indiana was eager, too. The Pacers hired him as coach, even though he had never coached at any level. "This guy is the epitome of everything I've tried to do here," said Pacers president Donnie Walsh. "When I started here, I wanted to see the high school, college, and professional basketball worlds come together, and Bird symbolizes that."

Bird's lack of experience didn't bother him. "I'm new at this [coaching] game, but I feel I can get the job done," he said. "I have all the confidence in the world that I'll be able to handle these guys and do the things that are necessary to win games." He did. "Basketball is not complicated, and Larry doesn't make it that way," said small forward/shooting guard Chris Mullin. "All of us appreciate his approach." The Pacers raced to 58 wins in 1997–98. Bird was NBA Coach of the Year. But the Chicago Bulls won the conference finals in seven games.

Larry Bird

CHICAGO VS. INDIANA
EASTERN CONFERENCE FINALS
GAME 4
MAY 25, 1998

TURNING THE TABLES

The Pacers trailed 94–93 with 2.9 seconds left. They had an inbounds play near half court. Reggie Miller curled toward the top of the key, where he met Michael Jordan. Jordan is famous for his game-winning shots. But that night, it was Miller's turn to play the hero. He brushed Jordan aside like an annoying insect and caught the inbounds pass. He launched a three-point shot as Jordan tried to catch up. It went in! In return, Jordan put up a slightly off-balance shot at the three-point line as time expired. It circled the rim and came out. Indiana won, 96–94.

The Pacers earned the second seed in the Eastern Conference the following season. They swept their first two playoff opponents. They faced the eighth-seeded Knicks in the conference finals. The Pacers lost three of the first five games by narrow margins. In Game 6, Miller ran out of gas. He scored just eight points. New York won 90–82 to take the series.

Bird coached Indiana to another good season in 1999–2000. Again, the Pacers faced the Knicks in the conference finals. Miller made sure that history would not repeat itself. He poured in 34 points as the Pacers won Game 6, 93–80 and the series, 4 games to 2. They were in the NBA Finals for the first time. They played the Los Angeles Lakers, who boasted both massive center Shaquille O'Neal and rising young superstar Kobe Bryant. The Pacers lost the series in six games. "They had a great team, and I'm not disputing that," said Miller. "But to get that close and not win will always be with all of us." Bird resigned as coach. He had back problems. The stress of coaching only made them worse.

The Pacers made the playoffs for the next three years. But they lost in the first round each time. New coach Rick Carlisle and players such as forwards Jermaine O'Neal and Ron Artest helped break this pattern in 2003–04. "Rick really knew his stuff, and he was good at coming up with plays and matchups for us," Miller said. "At the same time, we were working together and making our shots." The Pacers recorded their best season. They won 61 games. Artest was named NBA Defensive Player of the Year. But the team lost to the Detroit Pistons in the conference finals.

BY GEORGE, WE HAVE A GOOD TEAM

T he Pistons bounced the Pacers from the playoffs again in 2005. Miller retired. He played his entire career with Indiana. Tributes poured in. One was from Steve Alford. His NBA career had lasted just four years. He scored a total of 744 points in that time. Miller's lowest season point total was 800, in the twilight of his career. "It was a much better draft choice than drafting me," Alford said. "Reggie turned out not to be just a great pick, he turned out to be great for the state of Indiana." Indiana struggled for several seasons. The scoring of small forward Danny Granger was one of the few bright spots. Center Roy Hibbert was a force in the paint, which is the area around the basket from the free throw line to the end line.

The team drafted 6-foot-8 small forward/shooting guard Paul George in 2010. A scout predicted, "In five years, Paul George will be the best player to come out of this draft." Despite a 37–45 mark, Indiana returned to the playoffs. It lost in the first round. As George gained experience, Indiana's record improved. The Pacers went 42–24 in the lockout-shortened 2011–12 season. They lost to the Miami Heat in the conference semifinals. They did even better in the next two seasons. Indiana advanced to the conference finals. Both times the Heat scorched them. George remained upbeat. "The great thing is we're a young team, and we are past the building stage," he said. "The rate we are going, we will see championships soon."

INDIANA VS. DETROIT
NOVEMBER 19, 2004

BASKETBRAWL

Indiana held a 97–82 lead in a tense game. Less than a minute remained.
The Pacers' Ron Artest fouled Ben Wallace of the Pistons. The two players
started shoving each other. Teammates separated them. A Pistons fan
threw a cup of soda at Artest. He rushed into the stands. That ignited
fighting between spectators and players. A fan threw a heavy steel folding
chair at a player. It narrowly missed. Chuck Person, now a Pacers assistant
coach, said it was like being "trapped in a gladiator-type scene where the
fans were the lions, and we were just trying to escape with our lives." The
NBA suspended nine players. Artest's suspension lasted 86 games. It cost
him nearly $5 million of his salary.

JERMAINE O'NEAL
POWER FORWARD/CENTER
HEIGHT: 6-FOOT-11
PACERS SEASONS: 2000-08

YOUNGEST EVER

At just 17 years old, the Portland Trail Blazers selected Jermaine O'Neal 17th overall in the 1996 NBA Draft. By the time he played his first professional game he was 18 years and 53 days old. At that time, he was the youngest ever to play in an NBA game. O'Neal didn't appear ready. He started only 18 games in 4 years with Portland and only averaged nearly 4 points a game. He was traded to Indiana. There he found his game. O'Neal started all but one game his first season with Indiana and averaged nearly 13 points a game. In 2001-02, he was named the NBA's Most Improved Player. He made his first All-Star game that season. He followed that with five straight All-Star game appearances and mentions on three All-NBA teams. In eight seasons in Indiana, O'Neal averaged nearly 19 points and 10 rebounds a game.

During an off-season scrimmage while playing with the U.S. national team in 2014, George landed awkwardly on his leg and suffered a compound fracture. The injury sidelined him for nearly all the 2014–15 season. Indiana dipped to 38–44 and missed the playoffs. A healthy George returned to putting up big numbers the following season, and Indiana surged back. The Pacers added shooting guard Monta Ellis. George and Ellis led the Pacers to 45 wins The season also brought the addition of Myles Turner. He was an All-Rookie Second Team selection. The Toronto Raptors beat them in the playoffs, 4 games to 3.

That set the pattern for the next four seasons. The Pacers won between 42 and 48 games during that time. Each season they lost in the first round of the playoffs. Turner turned into a shot-blocking presence. Twice he led the league in blocked shots. The Pacers won just 34 games in 2020–21 and missed the playoffs. Point guard Malcolm Brogdon led two other players with averages of more than 20 points a game in his first season with the team.

Indiana took a step backward in 2021–22, losing their final 10 games to finish 25–57. But a late-season trade with Sacramento brought point/shooting guard Tyrese Haliburton to Indiana. He averaged more than 17 points and nearly 10 assists per game. The same trade netted shooting guard Buddy Hield, who averaged more than 18 points a game. "For a team trying to rebuild, it's hard to make a better move than the one the Pacers made here," wrote Rohan Nadkarni of Sports Illustrated. In addition to the mid-season acquistions, Indiana selected

Tyrese Haliburton

Arizona guard/forward Bennedict Mathurin with the sixth overall pick in the NBA Draft. He raised his scoring average from 10.8 points per game as a freshman to 17.7 points as a sophomore in the 2021-22 season.

James Naismith invented basketball in a Massachusetts gym in 1891. Nearly 30 years later, he watched an Indiana high school state championship game. "Basketball really had its origin in Indiana, which remains the center of the sport," he wrote afterward. "Hoosier hysteria" extends to all levels of basketball in the state. The Indiana University Hoosiers have won five NCAA Division I basketball titles. The Evansville Purple Aces boast five NCAA Division II crowns. The Pacers dominated the ABA. The "hysteria" even extends to Hollywood. Hoosiers is perhaps the ultimate underdog movie. It depicts a tiny Indiana high school that wins a state championship in the 1950s. There's only one gap in the state's rich basketball tradition: an NBA title. Fans hope that the Pacers will take care of that in the very near future.

Myles Turner

INDEX

Chuck Person